THE WEIGHT LOSS SURGERY COPING COMPANION

THE WEIGHT LOSS SURGERY COPING COMPANION

A PRACTICAL GUIDE FOR COPING WITH POST-SURGERY EMOTIONS

SECOND EDITION

Tanie Miller Kabala Ph.D.

ACKNOWLEDGMENTS

⁓ϲ

This book is dedicated to all of the weight loss surgery patients whom I have had the honor to work with and know. They have touched me with their genuineness, vulnerability, openness, and courage. I thank each of them for inspiring me, both personally and professionally. My hope is that others might be equally moved by their stories.

Please note that all names in this book have been changed to protect confidentiality.

INTRODUCTION

t is my pleasure to introduce you to the Weight Loss Surgery Coping
Companion, Second Edition. Let me begin by stating that I admire your
courage in pursuing this life-changing surgery, and I commend you for taking this important step in self-care.

I have the privilege of working daily with patients who have recently un-
dergone weight loss surgery. Following surgery, these courageous individuals
often experience a wide variety of emotions: emotions including loneliness,
anger, anxiety, depression, identity confusion, and the overwhelming urge to
overeat.

Many post-surgery patients tell me that they have never experienced these
feelings before, or at least have not felt them so intensely, because they had
previously used overeating to "numb out," "escape," "self-soothe," and simply
"make the feelings go away." These patients frequently come into my office
saying, "I have no idea how to cope without food!" This is why I created the
Weight Loss Surgery Coping Companion. In this resource guide, I help you
do two things: understand your experience of these emotions; and provide
specific, personalized strategies to allow you to cope with them in healthy,
effective ways. I specifically address loneliness, anger, anxiety, depression,
identity confusion ("Who am I?"), and the compulsion to overeat. My inten-
tion is that the guide provides you with strategies that you will use not only

following surgery, but also for a lifetime. All the best to you as you embark on this journey of nurturing and self-care.

Very sincerely yours,

Tanie Miller Kabala, Ph.D.

TABLE OF CONTENTS

CHAPTER 1

LIFE AFTER WEIGHT LOSS SURGERY

~⌒~

"The psychologist who evaluated me before surgery said that the surgery could be difficult emotionally, but I had no idea just how hard it would be. As the weight started coming off, I was excited and terrified all at once. There were so many feelings, and I no longer could binge to escape them. Sometimes I just wanted to go back to my old life- hiding away from the world in my apartment and just eating."

-Carrie

What is life like after weight loss surgery? Just as Carrie said, most people find it very complex- exciting, terrifying, full of new opportunities, *and* full of new emotional challenges. What are these challenges? In listening to the stories of my patients, I've found that they fall into three broad categories: the challenge of adjusting to a new body; the challenge of managing others' reactions to weight loss; and, of course, the challenge of adjusting to a brand new relationship with food.

<u>Adjusting to a new body</u>

Most of my weight loss surgery patients have shared that they've spent the majority of their lives overweight. Therefore, as Carrie said, weight loss after surgery can be simultaneously thrilling and terrifying: thrilling because of the "chance for a new life," and terrifying because of the new, anxiety-provoking opportunities it affords.

My patients frequently share that being overweight allowed them to "hide" from certain frightening experiences, such as dating, being physically intimate, making friends, and interviewing for jobs. My patient Ginny, who was both neglected by her parents and teased by her peers, said:

"I hid behind my fat all my life. Now that I've had surgery, I feel like I have no excuse not to 'put myself out there' and date. It's so scary. I have no idea how to date. I've never had a boyfriend….and I'm terrified of being rejected. I feel anxious about it all the time."

Similarly, Sara, a survivor of childhood sexual abuse, shared the following:

"I was sexually abused by my uncle from age four to age ten. I never wanted to be sexual since, and I think the fat protected me from that. Now I want a second chance at getting married, but I'm scared to death. I've never even kissed a boy."

Another client, Missy, shared the following:

"I'm 30 years old and still live with my parents. I have a college degree in speech pathology but have never worked. My excuse was that no one would hire me at my weight (450 pounds), but really, I was just afraid to work because I was afraid that no one would like me or that I would fail. Now that I've had the surgery, what is my excuse? I need to get over these fears."

Just like Ginny, Sara, and Missy, most of my patients report that having a "new body" means facing old fears- fears of intimacy, rejection, and vulnerability that developed from painful experiences in childhood or adolescence. Such experiences include abusive or neglectful parenting; physical, sexual, or emotional abuse; frequent moves; chaotic conditions at home (such as constant fighting); rejection from peers; and severe or chronic health issues.

In the chapters that follow, I offer techniques that will help you understand and cope with the feelings and situations associated with your "new body," feelings such as anxiety, depression, anger, loneliness, and identity confusion ("who am I now?"). By *developing insight* into your emotions and *taking action* to cope with them in healthy ways (using my Insight and Action, or INACT Technique), you will be equipped to fully experience life for the first time.

Managing Others' Reactions to Surgery and Weight Loss

Nearly all of my patients have shared that they have received "unique" reactions from others regarding their surgery and resulting weight loss: reactions born out of envy, resentment, or vulnerability. While friends and family members are often thrilled about a loved one's weight loss, there are instances in which the reactions are hurtful, stressful, or confusing. Kate, for example, shared that her best friend became very envious of her weight loss. This led to a rift in the friendship and significant sadness, loss, anger, and loneliness for Kate. Another patient, Sara, shared the following:

"I realized that I'd always bonded with two of my friends around eating and being fat together. When I couldn't overeat with them anymore, I felt really left out. They couldn't understand what I was going through."

Still another patient, Ginny, shared this experience:

"When I lost weight, my brother said to my sister, 'Now Ginny is the skinniest one in the family.' This did not go over well with my sister. Things are so tense between us now."

Finally, Vickie shared the following experience with her husband:

"My husband is getting really jealous and I don't know what to do. Last night he said, 'Who do you think you are in those tight jeans? Are you trying to find a new man or something?' He was jealous when we were dating, but I hadn't seen it in years. Makes me feel bad about the whole thing. I don't want to stop wearing my new clothes though, but I don't want him freaking out and making me feel bad."

Hurtful reactions are unfortunately a common part of the post-weight loss surgery experience. In the chapters that follow, I provide concrete strategies for understanding the feelings that such hurtful reactions can spawn (loneliness, anxiety, anger, depression, and identity confusion) and taking healthy action to reconcile them.

<u>Adjusting to a new relationship with food</u>

In my ten-plus years of working with weight loss surgery patients, I have learned that many have a long history of using overeating as a means of coping with challenging emotions. I frequently hear that these patients began overeating in childhood as a means to soothe painful emotions, and that this habit was maintained, and usually strengthened, into adulthood.

I often hear that my patients were abandoned or neglected by parents; abused physically, sexually, or emotionally; teased or ignored by peers or siblings; and exposed to chaotic conditions (e.g., divorce, constant fighting/yelling by parents and siblings, frequent moves). Additionally, I often hear that my patients felt as though their siblings were favored by parents, other family members, and members of the community. Within these painful environments, and without loving guidance, these patients understandably turned to food as a readily available means of coping. It was a survival mechanism that they desperately needed. As John shared:

"When I came home from middle school, I'd eat everything: peanut butter and jelly crackers, chips, Little Debbies, soda, and chocolate milk... it was how I relaxed." John continued this behavior into adulthood, leaving stressful meetings at work and "going straight to Dunkin' Donuts for coffee and a half dozen donuts."

Similarly, Vickie shared the following about her experience as a commuter in college:

"After a hard day, I'd just come home, get in my comfy clothes, and eat things like chips, microwave mac and cheese, and cupcakes. It was the only thing I knew to make me feel better."

Following weight loss surgery, when overeating is no longer a viable option because of the physical consequences (e.g., Dumping Syndrome), patients like Vickie are faced with the challenging task of finding new, healthy ways to cope with their emotions. This can feel completely overwhelming. As another patient, Evelyn, said:

"Yeah, before the surgery, at least I knew what to do when I felt stressed-eat. Now, I have no idea, so it's like a double-whammy- I feel stressed out to start, and helpless to do anything about it, which makes me even more stressed."

It was statements like this that motivated me to write this book. In the following chapters, you will (a) develop an increased understanding of your feelings following weight loss surgery and (b) identify concrete, personalized, *healthy* strategies for coping with them. We will focus on loneliness, anger, anxiety, depression, identity confusion, and the overwhelming desire to overeat.

In the next five chapters (those regarding loneliness, anger, anxiety, depression, and identity confusion), we will utilize the Insight and Action (INACT) Technique. This technique involves four steps that will allow you to both *understand* your emotions (Insight) and effectively *cope* with them (Action) *without using food.* Those four steps are:

1. Exploring your personal *experience* of the emotion in question, facilitated through real-life examples, thought-provoking questions, and writing exercises.

2. Exploring your personal *needs* related to that emotion, facilitated through thought-provoking questions and writing exercises.

3. Identifying *specific coping strategies* for addressing that emotion. A list of non-food related coping strategies is provided, and you will be encouraged to reflect on and *personalize* items on that list.

4. Recording your favorite coping strategies for each emotion on a "Coping Companion" list on page 87, for easy reference.

In the seventh chapter, *How to Cope with the Urge to Overeat*, I will introduce you to two techniques that I have developed: the Nourish Technique and the COPE Technique. The Nourish Technique is a mindfulness-based technique that will help you avoid emotional eating and nourish yourself both physically and emotionally. To summarize, the Nourish Technique will guide you through a series of questions including:

1. Are you physically or emotionally hungry?

2. If you are physically hungry, what exactly is your body craving right now?

3. If you are emotionally hungry, what are you truly wanting and needing right now?

4. If you are emotionally hungry, what could you do right now to address that need that does not involve food?

The second technique that we will personalize is the COPE technique. This technique can be used when you are feeling compelled to overeat but feel too tired or overwhelmed to walk through the NOURISH questions above. To summarize, COPE stands for **C**hange your environment; **O**pen up to someone; **P**ray, meditate or do a breathing exercise; and **E**xercise.

I'm so glad that you decided to take this important step in self-care with me. Let's get started.

CHAPTER 2

HOW TO COPE WITH LONELINESS

&

"After surgery, I felt horribly lonely. Not only
was I lacking in friendships and dating, but it
was also like I had lost my best friend- food."

-Kate

Loneliness is an extremely common emotion among post-surgery patients.
Many of my patients have made comments like that of Kate: that after
surgery, they are not only dissatisfied with their social lives, but also feel
as though they have lost the faithful and comforting friend that has been with
them since childhood- food. Kate talked about her loss in great depth:

"I remember being a little girl, coming home from school after another terrible bus ride where the kids teased me. They called me "Kate
the heavyweight," and loved to chant, "We hate Kate!" My parents
were divorced and my mom never paid any attention to me, so I'd just
go to my room, get in bed with the candy that I bought with money
from my grandparents, and read. This continued all through school
and into college, where I requested a single dorm room so that nobody

would see how much I ate. Things just cycled and I was more and more alone, away from people and hidden away with my food."

Like Kate, many weight loss surgery patients have a long history of loneliness. Some experienced neglect and abandonment from parents and spent much of their childhoods alone. Others experienced painful rejection from siblings, kids in the neighborhood, and classmates. Many learned to use food as a means to escape from these painful circumstances- and found themselves increasingly alienated from others in the process.

Perhaps you have had similar experiences. Perhaps you too learned to *survive* your painful circumstances by using food as a coping mechanism- a means of escaping from the pain. Let me assure you that there is no shame in this- in fact, it is evidence of your *resilience*. As a child and/or adolescent, you found the best means that you could to cope with your challenging circumstances. Now, however, you have the opportunity to replace those old coping mechanisms with new, healthier mechanisms. Let's get started, using the INACT Technique:

INACT Exercise #1: Gaining Insight Into Your Personal Experience of Loneliness

Using the questions below as a guide, let's learn about your feelings of loneliness. There is space for your answers on the following pages. Feel free to write, draw, or even make a collage of pictures expressing yourself. This is an opportunity to identify, clarify, and truly *experience* your feelings, rather than avoiding or numbing them. I think you will find that truly experiencing and expressing your emotions is a big step in the healing process. As you allow the feelings to wash over you and move them onto the paper, you may experience a sense of purging, relief, and understanding. Remember, there is no wrong way to do this exercise- your self-expression, in any form, is exactly right.

* What makes me feel lonely?
* When do I usually feel lonely?

* Are there certain places that make me feel lonely?
* Are there certain people who leave me feeling lonely?
* When have I felt lonely in the past?
* What words best describe my loneliness?
* Is there someone or something that I am missing?

My Journaling Page

My Journaling Page

INACT Exercise #2: What Do You Need in Order to Feel Less Lonely?

Let's take a close look at this question: "What do *I* need to feel less lonely?" In my work, I have repeatedly noted the following phenomenon: that for post-surgery patients, the notion of making their own needs a top priority is a foreign concept. Why? Many patients have shared that because their parents did not attend to their needs, they came to feel that those needs did not matter. Many patients have also shared that they tend to put others' needs before theirs, hoping to win love and approval. Because of these dynamics, many of my patients have no idea what their needs are. One day, when I asked my patient Sara what she was needing, she looked at me blankly and said, "I have no idea. No one has ever asked me that before."

Perhaps you feel the same way- unclear about your needs and wants because they were not recognized by your parents. Perhaps you feel as though your wants and needs don't matter and that others' needs should come first.

Please read this closely: this is absolutely not the case. Your needs *do* matter. No parent or other caregiver, under any circumstances, should make a child feel as if his or her needs are unimportant. If you were neglected, mistreated, or abused, it was your caregivers' issues that were the cause. If your caregiver(s) did any of these things, *rest assured that this is not because of anything you did, didn't do, were, or were not. Like all children, you were innocent and deserved unconditional love, nurturing, and attention.* I encourage you to re-read this many times if it's a new concept. Also, I encourage you to respond to your experience with lots of *compassion*, rather than self-judgment or criticism.

Now, let's get to work on making your needs a top priority. Think again about your feelings of loneliness. What do you need in order to feel less lonely? Use the following pages to express your needs, using the following insight-oriented questions as a guide:

* Do I need to connect more often with friends and family?
* Do I need to find a community of which to be a part?
* Do I need support for my post-surgery experience?

- Do I need a pet?
- Do I need to call someone in particular? Get together with someone in particular?
- Do I need to get out among people, without the pressure of a one-on-one interaction? If so, where would I like to go?
- Do I need to reconcile an issue with someone in my life so that we can reconnect?
- Do I need to start the process of preparing to date?

My Journaling Page

My Journaling Page

INACT Exercise #3: Taking Action to Address Loneliness

Now that you've gained insight about your feelings and needs, let's start taking action by pinpointing some *specific* things that you can do to cope with your feelings of loneliness. Below you'll find a list of strategies that my patients have found helpful. You can read each strategy and personalize it in the space provided, using my prompts as a guide. Then, go back and circle **the strategies that really appeal to you, bearing in mind the needs that you identified earlier.**

1. *Join a support group.* Many of my patients have addressed loneliness by attending Overeaters Anonymous meetings, getting involved in weight loss surgery support groups, and joining psychotherapy groups. You might find great comfort and connection in talking with others who have been through what you've been through. You can go to Oa.org to learn about the Overeaters Anonymous program and to find a group near you. Also, your surgeon is a good person to ask about local weight loss surgery support groups. Finally, many of my patients have found online support forums, such as the ones at ObesityHelp. com, extremely helpful during their recovery periods. Below, write down any support groups that appeal to you:

   _____

   _____

   _____

2. *Work with a therapist* who has experience working with post-surgery patients. A good therapist will provide you with kindness and support, and will help you better understand your pre and post surgery experience. If you would like to find a therapist but are not sure how, please refer to page 90 of this book. There, I have listed a number of resources for finding a qualified professional.

3. *Join a group that is a good fit for your interests.* Affiliating with a group is a great way to address loneliness. Not sure what type of group would be a good fit for you? This is not uncommon among post-surgery patients. I have found that many of my patients have not had the opportunity to reflect on their true interests and passions-they have been investing their energy trying to avoid punishment or gain approval from others. To explore your interests, I recommend looking at Meetup.org, a site dedicated to helping like-minded people connect through small group meetings or "meetups." Browse the options with an open mind and see what appeals to you. There are meetup groups for just about anything you can think of- knitters, board game players, lovers of Broadway musicals, walkers, dog lovers, acoustic guitar players, vegetarian cooks, sci-fi lovers, French speakers, health and wellness advocates, etc. Even if you don't feel ready to join a group, exploring your interests in a non-judgmental way is a great place to start. What groups might be a good fit for you?

_____

_____

_____

4. *Reach out to a family member, friend, or other loved one by phone or in person.* Are there specific friends or loved ones whom you would like to call, visit, or connect with in some other way? Write their names down below, along with how you'd like to connect with them:

_____

_____

_____

If you aren't able to identify anyone, you're not alone. I have learned that many post-surgery patients struggle with identifying "safe" others with whom to share their feelings. Frequently, they tell me that they "can't trust anyone" or "don't want to burden anybody with my problems." These feelings often stem from painful past experiences, such as being punished for expressing feelings as a child, or from being rejected for expressing emotions to a partner or friend. If you struggle with such feelings, I encourage you to enlist the help of a therapist. He or she can help you identify safe others with whom to share your feelings. I have found that when I help my patients identify safe others with whom to share, they are often pleasantly surprised by the warm reception that they receive. They also learn that self-disclosure (of both "the good and the bad") with a caring person builds connection and intimacy.

5. ***Get a pet.*** Studies have shown that individuals with pets report less loneliness, depression, and anxiety than those without. If you're open to getting a pet, think about what type would best fit your lifestyle. Many of my patients have greatly benefited from the comforting relationships they've developed with their dogs, cats, chinchillas, guinea pigs, fish, and even indoor rabbits and pot-belly pigs. Are there any pets that are of interest to you? If so, list them below, along with the names of local pet stores or animal shelters that you could visit to gather more information:

_____

_____

_____

6. ***If you are a spiritual or religious person, consider visiting or joining a church, synagogue, or other such organization.*** These can offer great opportunities to connect with like-minded others. Many offer both small group experiences (e.g., women's and men's groups, volunteer groups, book clubs, music groups) and large group experiences (e.g., worship, picnics, dinners). Are there any such places that are of interest

to you? Are there small or large group experiences that appeal to you? List them below:

_____

_____

_____

7. ***Take a class.*** Consider taking a class that focuses on something that you are genuinely interested in- and again, if you're not sure what you're interested in, that's okay- just engage yourself in a process of exploration. Imagine yourself taking a jewelry making class….a dance class….a yoga class…..a meditation class…..a cooking class….a singing class…..a computer literacy class…..an exercise class…..an acting class…..a calligraphy class….a photography class. These are all examples of classes that my post surgery patients have pursued. Classes are frequently offered by community centers, local college and universities, YMCAs, art studios, and dance studios. What might you enjoy?

_____

_____

_____

8. ***Journal.*** Buy yourself journal that you find appealing and start a regular practice of writing down your thoughts and feelings. Make this journal your companion in the post-surgery process- the holder of your thoughts, feelings, wants, and needs. Some of my patients have also benefited from sharing their feelings with other patients via online post-surgery forums. Whatever the forum, many find it healthy and relieving to vent their feelings through writing. Are you interested in journaling in a notebook or via an online forum? Write any thoughts below:

_____

_____

_____

9. ***Volunteer for a cause or agency that you believe in.*** Volunteering allows you to connect with like-minded others while doing something meaningful; and studies have shown that volunteering is directly linked with emotional well-being. What are some possibilities for volunteering? You could walk the dogs at an animal shelter, help maintain a state park, build a relationship with a child through Big Brothers/Big Sisters, teach someone to read at an adult literacy center, visit with patients at a hospital, teach a Sunday school class at church, help kids with homework at a child care center, serve food at a meal kitchen, deliver meals to shut-ins through Meals on Wheels, or give tours at a museum. There are many possibilities, and <u>Volunteermatch. org</u>, <u>allforgood.org</u>, and <u>Unitedway.org</u> are great websites for finding volunteer opportunities. What volunteer activities might be a good fit for you? Jot down any ideas below:

_____

_____

_____

10. ***Engage in a nurturing self-care activity.*** Sometimes we feel lonely but don't have the energy to "get out there" and engage with others. If you're feeling that way, try coping with these feelings by *caring for yourself.* Try doing something that will make you feel nurtured-watch a comedy, do some gentle yoga, take a walk in nature, read a book you've been wanting to read, or get a massage, facial, manicure, pedicure, or other treatment. Send yourself the message that you are valuable person who deserves caring. What are three nurturing activities that you might enjoy?

_____

_____

_____

INACT Exercise #4: Getting Organized

Now, let's get you completely prepared to take action by creating your personal coping card for addressing loneliness. Below, write down all of the strategies that you have identified as potentially helpful for coping with loneliness (those that you circled above). I have included five spaces, but feel free to include more:

1. _____
2. _____
3. _____
4. _____
5. _____

I hope that you now feel well-equipped to take action against feelings of loneliness. Now, let's turn our attention to feelings of anger.

CHAPTER 3

HOW TO COPE WITH ANGER

⟡

"After the surgery, these intense feelings of anger
came up from out of nowhere. I completely lost
it on my mother one night at a family dinner. I
was screaming and swearing and my sister had to
hold me back. I was completely out of control."

-Sara

Like Sara, many of my post-surgery patients are surprised to find themselves overwhelmed by intense feelings of anger. Because they suddenly can't use food to escape from their anger, it comes out *full force*. They are confronted with intense anger towards their mothers, fathers, siblings, friends, classmates, uncles, aunts, cousins, grandparents, teachers, coaches, bosses, co-workers, husbands, wives, significant others, spiritual and religious leaders, and, unfortunately, themselves. They are angry about events both recent and distant- events from yesterday, events from 50 years ago.

In my work, I have learned that my post-surgery patients have very good reasons to be angry. Many have been seriously mistreated, both physically and emotionally, by people close to them. To make matters worse, many patients were taught that their anger- which was completely justified- was not okay. For example, Sara recalled that her mother, who was emotionally abusive, shamed her anytime that she expressed angry or sad emotions. Her mother would shout, "Shut your mouth! You're a lucky girl and should be happy!" Other patients have come to equate anger with "being out of control," because their caregivers had anger management problems. They therefore have come to suppress their angry feelings, trying desperately to keep from losing control themselves.

Have you experienced this as well? Do you have a lot of anger inside? Were you raised to feel that it was not acceptable for you to be angry? Were you raised to be afraid of anger? If so, know that you are not alone and that this can be successfully addressed. Please hear me out on this: **it is okay to be angry. Anger is a normal, healthy, and adaptive emotion.** Our goal is to help you understand your anger, recognize that it's okay to feel it, and identify healthy strategies for expressing and coping with it. Let's get started.

INACT Exercise #1: Gaining Insight Into Your Personal Experience of Anger

As we did with your feelings of loneliness, use the following pages (and feel free to use additional paper) to gain insight into your feelings of anger. Feel free to express anything you're feeling. Again, you can write, draw, make a collage of pictures, or express yourself in any other way that feels right. This is another opportunity to move your feelings out of your mind and onto the paper, which often provides a sense of purging and relief. Remember, there is no wrong way to do this exercise. Your self-expression, in any form, is exactly right. You can use the questions below to guide you:

- At whom am I angry? Why? What would I like to say to him/her/them?
- When have I been angry in the past?
- What words best describe my anger?
- Where do I feel the anger in my body?
- How has anger been handled in my family?
- What do I feel like doing with this anger?

My Journaling Page

My Journaling Page

INACT Exercise #2: What Do You Need in Order to Cope with Your Feelings of Anger?

Just as we did with your feelings of loneliness, let's take some time to determine what you need in order to cope with your angry feelings. It may be very difficult for you to figure this out. As I've mentioned, many of my post-surgery patients have not been taught to focus on their own needs. If you're having trouble determining your needs, use these questions as a guide:

* Do I need to "get my feelings out" somehow?
* Do I need to express my anger to someone?
* Would it feel good to vent my feelings physically? For example, might it feel good to yell, punch something safe (like a punching bag or pillow), or exercise?
* Do I need to take myself out of a relationship that perpetuates feelings of anger (e.g., a relationship in which I am taken advantage of or abused)?
* Do I need to take myself out of a situation that perpetuates feelings of anger (e.g., a situation where I am not appreciated)?

Now, in the space that follows, do your best to write what you specifically need to manage your anger in a healthy way. For example, "Stop babysitting for June unless she starts paying me," "Take that self-defense class I've been thinking about."

My Journaling Page

My Journaling Page

My Journaling Page

INACT Exercise #3: Taking Action to Address Anger

Now that you've gained insight into your feelings and needs, let's start taking action by pinpointing some *specific* things that you can do to cope with your feelings of anger. Below you'll find a list of strategies that my patients have found helpful. You can read each strategy and personalize it in the space provided. Then, go back and circle the strategies that really appeal to you, bearing in mind the needs that you identified above through our insight-building questions.

1. *Vent your anger physically.* Many of my patients have found this to be very helpful. One patient hung a punching bag in her garage and uses it whenever she needs to vent anger in a healthy way. Others have opted to take self-defense classes like Tae Kwon Do, Karate, and RAD (Rape Aggression Defense). Such classes not only allow you to vent your feelings, but also help you develop physical strength and feelings of empowerment and control. Engaging in other forms of exercise, such as walking, running, yoga, or biking can also help in the coping process. Be sure to consult your doctor before engaging in one of these activities, especially if your surgery was very recent or if you have other health issues. What physical means of venting your anger might work for you?

    _____

    _____

    _____

2. *Express your anger through art.* It can be incredibly healing to vent your anger through painting, drawing, dancing, or singing. One of my patients finds it helpful to get in her car, turn up the volume on a meaningful song, and sing at the top of her lungs. Another finds a movement class called "Shake Your Soul" very powerful. Others

have found it helpful to paint, sculpt, and draw to express their anger. Below, list any artistic means of expressing anger that appeal to you:

_____

_____

_____

3. ***Write a letter to someone with whom you're angry.*** You don't have to send the letter (this is something that you could explore with a therapist), but just getting your feelings out can be very therapeutic. I frequently find that my patients keep their angry feelings inside, rather than directing them "out where they belong." This can lead to depression, anxiety, and fatigue. What feelings might you be turning inwards? Write them down below, along with the names of anyone to whom you would like to write a letter:

_____

_____

_____

4. ***Vent your feelings verbally to someone supportive and caring.*** This might be a therapist (and tips for finding a therapist can be found on page 90), friend, family member, partner, or religious/spiritual leader. To whom might you like to vent your feelings?

_____

_____

_____

5. ***Consider addressing a person or situation that is at the root of your anger.*** This can be extremely helpful, as it can provide a sense of empowerment, control, and, importantly, closure. Such a step can be very scary and complicated though, so I recommend exploring this with a therapist. He or she can help you clarify your feelings, explore

options, and determine likely consequences. Are there any anger-provoking people or situations in your life right now? How might you address them? Write your thoughts below:

_____

_____

_____

6. ***Journal.*** As with your feelings of loneliness, I encourage you to buy yourself a journal that you love and use it to express your angry feelings. Don't hold back! Write whatever comes to mind, moving the feelings out of your body and onto the paper. Are there any anger-provoking situations that you would like to journal about?

_____

_____

_____

7. ***Have a ceremony.*** As I mentioned earlier, many of my patients have good reasons to be angry at people who have mistreated them (or are mistreating them currently). Some of these patients have found it very therapeutic to have a ceremony in which they rid themselves of objects symbolic of a person or relationship that has been harmful. One client had a ceremonial burning of her father's shoes since they reminded her of his angry footsteps. Another burned all pictures and letters of an ex who had abused her. Still another had a ceremonial "pouring" in which she poured alcohol down a drain, symbolic of putting her mother's alcoholism behind her. All found that these ceremonies were empowering and left them feeling less angry and more peaceful. What kind of ceremony might be empowering to you?

_____

_____

_____

8. ***Meditate.*** A growing body of research suggests that regular meditation and/or yoga can be a highly effective means of coping with difficult emotions such as anger. You might consider taking a meditation or yoga class at your local YMCA, yoga studio, or fitness center. Also, you might try a meditation, yoga, or deep breathing DVD or CD. My meditation and relaxation CD, *Rest and Restore: Meditations and Relaxation Exercises for Stress-Relief, Mindfulness, and Peaceful Sleep* is available for digital download on iTunes, Google Play, and other major distribution outlets; and in hard-copy format at drtaniekabala. com and Amazon.com. You might also try a smartphone meditation app, which can be used just about anywhere. Many apps offer 5, 10, 15, or 20 minute meditations. My meditation app, *Present and Peaceful,* is available for both Android and Apple smartphones and offers a mindfulness meditation, a walking meditation, and a five minute restorative meditation.

If you don't have time to take a full class or do an entire DVD on a given day, or if you don't have access to apps, you can try carving out some time (even five minutes) to do some basic, self-guided breath work. Three examples of simple breath work that you can do anytime and anywhere are:

   a. **I Am Relaxed.** For this breath work, sit comfortably, close your eyes, and breathe in and out normally. On your inhale, silently recite, "I am…" and on your exhale, recite, "relaxed." You may use any other mantra that is meaningful to you. Some mantras my clients have used are, "Healing in (on the inhalation)…….pain out (on the exhalation)," and "Love in (to self)……love out (to others)." Continue this for five to twenty minutes (or longer if you'd like).

   b. **Breath Attention.** For this practice, sit comfortably, close your eyes, and breathe in and out normally. Simply pay attention to your breath. Note where you feel the breath in your body. Do you feel it filling your lungs? Do you feel it in your belly? Leaving your nostrils? Whenever your mind wanders, just return to attending to your breath. Continue this practice for five to twenty minutes.

c. **Five Senses Meditation.** Close your eyes. Take five to ten calming breaths. Breathe in through your nose and out through your mouth. On the inhale, silently say to yourself, "I am." On the exhale, say to yourself, "Relaxed." Next, take a few minutes to notice each of your five senses. Silently say to yourself:

"I hear _____" Simply notice the sounds around you.

"I feel _____" Simply notice any physical sensations in your body.

"I smell _____" Simply notice any smells in the air.

"I taste _____" Simply notice any tastes in your mouth.

"I see _____" Open your eyes and notice what you see around you.

Repeat as many times as you'd like, for five to twenty minutes. Finish with five more calming breaths.

Do any of the meditative practices above appeal to you?

_____

_____

_____

INACT Exercise #4: Getting Organized

Now, let's get you completely prepared to take action by creating your personalized list of strategies for addressing anger. Below, write down all of the strategies that you have identified as potentially helpful for coping with anger (those that you circled above). I have included five spaces, but feel free to include more:

1. _____
2. _____
3. _____
4. _____
5. _____

Now you have a tangible list of strategies that you can use if you're feeling angry. I hope that you find them very useful, and that you turn to them whenever needed. Next, let's focus our attention on the experience of anxiety.

CHAPTER 4

HOW TO COPE WITH ANXIETY

~~

"After the surgery, I felt extremely agitated
and stressed. I just didn't know what to
do without food to help me relax."

-John

John, like many post-surgery patients, arrived at my office overwhelmed with anxiety. He talked at length about how soothing and comforting food had been to him since adolescence- and how very difficult it was to de-stress without it. As described earlier, John recalled coming from home from middle school each day (where he "felt like an outsider"), sitting on the couch, turning on the TV, and eating "everything: peanut butter and jelly crackers, chips, Little Debbies, soda, and chocolate milk." "It was how I relaxed," he said. John continued this behavior into adulthood, leaving stressful meetings at work and "going straight to Dunkin' Donuts for coffee and a half dozen donuts." After his LAP-BAND surgery, John found himself at a loss as to how to cope with anxiety without overeating.

Perhaps you feel like John: full of anxiety and not knowing how to cope without food. Again, trust me when I say that you are not alone. Rest assured that you **can** learn to cope in more healthy ways. Let's get started.

INACT Exercise #1: Gaining Insight into Your Personal Experience of Anxiety

In my work as a clinical psychologist, I have learned that a patient's anxiety often reflects the fact that she is struggling with **many** difficult feelings all at one time. I often tell clients that anxiety is not one emotion, but the manifestation of many thoughts, feelings, and experiences that need to be identified and resolved.

Vickie, for example, came to me feeling very anxious after her surgery. Our work revealed that she was worried about losing her job, worried that she would "gain all the weight back," and worried that she would never marry and "be alone forever." She was also very angry at her mother, sister, and a friend who had betrayed her. All of these feelings, several of which she'd been unaware, were "like a tangled knot in my stomach." Uncovering these feelings gave Vickie a sense of self-knowledge and control, and provided direction for the work that we would do together.

What unresolved thoughts and feelings might be underlying your anxiety? Is there fear? Anger? Sadness? Disappointment? Guilt? Write them down on the pages that follow. Do not censor your words- just allow them to flow naturally, out of your body and onto the paper.

My Journaling Page

My Journaling Page

INACT Exercise #2: What Do You Need in Order to Feel Less Anxious?

As with your feelings of loneliness and anger, let's take some time to determine what you personally need in order to reduce your anxiety. Again, it may be very difficult for you to determine this, as you may not have been taught to focus on your own needs. If you're having difficulty, use these questions as a guide:

* Do I need to take time to relax my body and/or my mind?
* Do I need to talk to someone, to help sort out my thoughts and feelings?
* Do I need to slow down?
* Do I need to simplify?
* Do I need support? From whom?
* Do I need to extricate myself from an anxiety-provoking situation or relationship?
* Do I need to take some things off of my plate?
* Do I need to say no to something or somebody?

Now, do your best to write below what you specifically need to reduce your anxiety (e.g., "Step down from one of the committees I'm on at the school," "Limit my exposure to a certain person who makes me feel anxious."):

My Journaling Page

My Journaling Page

My Journaling Page

INACT Exercise #3: Taking Action to Address Anxiety

Now that you've gained insight into your feelings and needs, let's start taking action by pinpointing some *specific* things that you can do to cope with your feelings of anxiety. Below you'll find a list of strategies that my patients have found helpful. You can read each strategy and personalize it in the space provided. Then, go back and circle the strategies that really appeal to you, bearing in mind the needs that you identified earlier through our insight-building exercises.

1. *Meditate.* Recent research strongly suggests that meditation (and the breath work done in yoga) is a highly effective tool in treating anxiety. You might consider taking a meditation or yoga class at your local YMCA, yoga studio, or fitness studio; or doing a meditation, yoga, or deep breathing DVD or CD. My meditation and relaxation CD, *Rest and Restore: Meditations and Relaxation Exercises for Stress-Relief, Mindfulness, and Peaceful Sleep* is available for digital download on iTunes, Google Play, and other major distribution outlets; and in hardcopy format at drtaniekabala.com and Amazon.com. You might also try a smartphone meditation app, which you can use almost anywhere. My meditation app, *Present and Peaceful,* is available for both Android and Apple smartphones and offers a mindfulness meditation, a walking meditation, and a five minute restorative meditation.

   If you face time restrictions, or if you don't have access to apps, I encourage you to take a few minutes each day (even five minutes) to do some basic, self-guided breath work. Again, here are three meditation practices that you can do anytime and anywhere:

   a. **I Am Relaxed.** For this breath work, sit comfortably, close your eyes, and breathe in and out normally. On your inhale, silently recite, "I am…" and on your exhale, recite, "relaxed." You may use any other mantra that is meaningful to you. Some mantras my clients have used are, "Healing in (on the inhalation)…….pain out (on the exhalation)," and "Love in (to self)……love out (to others)." Continue for five to twenty minutes.

b. **Breath Attention.** For this practice, sit comfortably, close your eyes, and breathe in and out normally. Simply pay attention to your breath. Note where you feel the breath in your body. Do you feel it filling your lungs? Do you feel it in your belly? Leaving your nostrils? Whenever your mind wanders, just return to observing your breath. Continue for five to twenty minutes.

c. **Five Senses Meditation.** Close your eyes. Take five to ten calming breaths. Breathe in through your nose and out through your mouth. On the inhale, silently say to yourself, "I am." On the exhale, say to yourself, "Relaxed." Next, take a minute to notice each of your five senses. Silently say to yourself:

"I hear _____" Simply notice the sounds around you.

"I feel _____" Simply notice any physical sensations in your body.

"I smell _____" Simply notice any smells in the air.

"I taste _____" Simply notice any tastes in your mouth.

"I see _____" Open your eyes and notice what you see around you.

Repeat as many times as you'd like, for five to twenty minutes. Finish with five more calming breaths.

Do any of the meditative practices above appeal to you?

_____

_____

_____

2. ***Clarify, vent, and address your feelings with a supportive person.***
    As mentioned earlier, I've found that anxiety often results from having many thoughts and feelings weighing upon you simultaneously. If you feel this way, I strongly encourage you to talk with a therapist. He or she can help you identify and clarify your feelings, problem solve, and make action plans (again, tips for finding a therapist can be found on page 90). To cite my previous example, I helped Vickie identify why she was angry at her mother, encouraged her to vent her feelings in our sessions, helped her set healthy boundaries, and provided her with effective communication techniques to use within the relationship. We did similar work with the other issues that were causing her anxiety; and soon, Vickie felt more relaxed, empowered, and in-control.

    You might also consider sharing your thoughts and feelings with a supportive friend or family member. Doing so might allow you to feel understood and heard, and could foster feelings of connection. With whom might you share your thoughts and feelings? A therapist? A friend or family member? Another trusted source?

    _____

    _____

    _____

3. ***Consider addressing any situation that is contributing to your anxiety.*** Julie, one of my patients, recognized through our work together that her relationship with her mother was causing her tremendous

anxiety. She shared that her mother had always been very critical and harsh with her (especially about her weight) and said, "I just can't relax when I'm with her- I know she's judging me." We discussed ways that she could set healthy boundaries and protect herself from this anxiety-provoking relationship. She learned to "say no" to her mother, limit their interactions, and assert herself when criticized. According to Julie, these boundaries "made me feel more in-control and way less anxious."

Some of my other patients have changed jobs upon recognizing the inordinate amount of anxiety that their work situation was causing. Still others have addressed anxiety-provoking romantic relationships. What relationships and/or situations are causing you anxiety? How might you address them in ways that would reduce your anxiety? Write your thoughts below. If this is hard to determine, I encourage you to consider talking with a therapist, friend, family member, or other trusted source.

_____

_____

_____

4. ***Say "no" when you need to.*** Many of my post-surgery patients find it difficult to say no. Why? As my patient Gina put it, "I want to be liked and am afraid of disappointing people." Gina recently recognized that she was overextending herself at church, "stressing myself out" with several leadership positions because she wanted the approval of the pastor and church members. Through our work together, Gina addressed her feelings of "wanting to be liked," discovered activities that are truly fulfilling to her, and found the courage to step down from one of her church posts. Are you overcommitted right now? If so, take a few moments to reflect on what would feel good to let go of. What could you say no to right now? How might you go about doing that?

_____

_____

_____

5. ***Engage in soothing, self-nurturing activities.*** I've found that one of the best ways to curb anxiety is to slow down and attend to yourself. As I've mentioned, this is a foreign concept to many of my post-surgery patients. Is it a foreign concept to you? If so, I encourage you to reflect on what might feel soothing to you. Do you need to slow down? Do you simply need to rest? Would you like to sit down in a quiet place and call a friend? Would a massage (or simply sitting in a massage chair) feel good? How about a warm bath or shower? Would it feel soothing to read a good book or magazine with a cup of tea? How about a walk in nature? Would you enjoy purchasing a bird feeder and watching the birds outside? Take a few moments to think: "What would feel soothing and relaxing to me?" and write your ideas down below.

_____

_____

_____

6. ***Do Progressive Muscle Relaxation (PMR).*** PMR is a wonderful stress-relief technique that involves sitting or lying comfortably and then contracting and relaxing the major muscle groups, one after another. This technique is so relaxing that I've actually had patients fall asleep when we've done it in my office. You can find a PMR script on page 91. PMR DVDs and CDs are also available at most major bookstores and at Amazon.com; and a PMR is included on my meditation CD, *Rest and Restore: Meditations and Relaxation Exercises for Stress-Relief, Mindfulness, and Peaceful Sleep,* which is available digitally on iTunes, Google Play, and other digital download distribution sites; and as a hard-copy CD at drtaniekabala.com and Amazon.com. You might also use a smartphone app to do PMR exercises. My relaxation app, *Rest and Restore,* includes a guided PMR, along with a guided beach imagery exercise and a five minute mindfulness exercise. *Rest and Restore* is available for both Android and Apple smartphones. Is

PMR something that you'd like to try? Would you like to try a DVD, CD or app? Write any thoughts below:

_____

_____

_____

INACT Exercise #4: Getting Organized

Now, let's create your personalized list of strategies for addressing anxiety. Below, write down all of the strategies that you have identified as potentially helpful (those that you circled above). I have included five spaces, but feel free to include more:

1. _____
2. _____
3. _____
4. _____
5. _____

I hope that you now have a better understanding of your anxious feelings AND a concrete plan for addressing them. Next, let's focus on the experience of depression.

CHAPTER 5

HOW TO COPE
WITH DEPRESSION

~⌒~

"Before I got the surgery, I thought it was going to
change everything. You know, make me totally
happy. But after the surgery, I realized that
although weight was coming off, I was still the
same: still lonely, still unhappy. This made me
totally depressed. I didn't want to get out of bed."

-Jean

Many patients confront depression at some point in their post-surgery journey. Some, like Jean, are deeply saddened to find that the surgery has not provided speedy relief from many of their troubles. Others, like my patient Shannon, experience depression because "that comforting indulgence of food is no longer an option." Still others have struggled with depression all of their lives. As I previously mentioned, many weight loss surgery patients have complicated and painful histories- histories including neglect, abuse, alienation, loneliness, rejection, and abandonment. "I've always had bouts of depression," Sara said during our first meeting, "Now I'm just a depressed person who weighs less."

Are you going through a bout of depression right now? Do you feel like you're "on the edge?" Have you experienced depression in the past? If so, you are not alone. Nearly all of my patients have experienced some level of depression at some point in the post-surgery process. The great news is that you've gotten this book and are taking steps to care for yourself. Depression is highly treatable. Let's get started.

INACT Exercise #1: Gaining Insight into Your Personal Experience of Depression

Let's begin by looking at the symptoms of depression:

1. Feelings of sadness, emptiness, or hopelessness
2. Sleeping more or less than usual
3. Significantly increased or decreased appetite
4. Loss of pleasure in previously enjoyed activities
5. Fatigue
6. Difficulty concentrating
7. Agitation
8. Suicidal thoughts

Are you experiencing any of these symptoms? Write any observations down below:

_____

_____

_____

If you are, in fact, experiencing any of the symptoms mentioned above, I would like to encourage you to consult with a family doctor, psychiatrist, or psychologist. These individuals can help you determine if you are experiencing a depressive episode and explore treatment options with you. As I've mentioned earlier, resources for finding a therapist can be found on page 90.

INACT Exercise #2: What Do You Need in Order to Feel Less Depressed?

In conjunction with a psychiatric/psychological consultation, let's initiate some self-care by helping you reflect on what you personally need in order to reduce your depressive feelings. Again, it may be very difficult for you to determine this, as you may not have been taught to focus on your own needs. If you're having difficulty, use these questions as a guide:

* Do I need to get out more often? If so, when and where?
* Do I need more social support? From whom?
* Do I need to take better care of myself? If so, what exactly do I need? More sleep? More exercise? More healthy snacks and meals?
* Do I need to extricate myself from a situation or relationship that makes me feel depressed?

Now, do your best to write what you specifically need in order to feel less depressed (e.g., "Get out of the house more often," "Join the YMCA and exercise a few times each week," "Have groceries delivered weekly," "Stop spending time with Chris- I always feel down afterwards.").

_____

_____

_____

INACT Exercise #3: Taking Action to Address Your Feelings of Depression

Now, let's pinpoint some *specific* things that you can do to cope with depressive feelings. Below you'll find a list of strategies that my patients have found helpful. You can read each strategy and personalize it in the space provided. Then, go back and circle the strategies that really appeal to you, bearing in mind the needs that you identified earlier.

1. ***Exercise.*** Exercise has the immediate physiological effect of improving mood via the release of endorphins. Although it may be the absolute *last* thing you feel like doing, I strongly encourage you to engage in some form of exercise if you are experiencing depressive symptoms. With your doctor's approval, take a brisk walk, do an exercise DVD, turn on your favorite upbeat CD and dance around the room, swim, turn on a fitness channel and try an exercise program, take a class, or engage in any form of physical activity that appeals to you (or is at least "okay"). A psychiatrist once said to me, "After therapy and medication, exercise is the single best thing you can do to relieve depression."

   If you're having trouble getting motivated, *really* try to focus on the mood boost you'll experience when you're done. Also, if you're comfortable, enlist the help of a loved one to help motivate you. As Suzanne said, "I just couldn't get up the motivation to exercise on my own. I used to call my friend and say, 'Tell me to put on my sneakers' and she would. This was the only way that I could get going." Whatever it takes, I strongly encourage you to make exercise part of your weekly routine. It will be worth it! And remember: any amount of exercise, even just five minutes, is better than none. Now take a moment and jot down a few forms of exercise you might be willing to try this week:

   _____

   _____

   _____

2. ***Go out.*** Again, although it might be the absolute last thing you feel like doing (and you may have to muster all of the energy you have), I strongly encourage you to get out of the house when you're feeling depressed. My patients tell me, nearly without fail, that their depression

improves when they go and do almost anything. Some "outings" that have helped my patients are:

    a. Browsing in a bookstore or craft store
    b. Walking in a park or simply sitting on a bench and breathing fresh air
    c. Going to a movie, concert, or show
    d. Visiting a loved one
    e. Going to church or synagogue
    f. Walking on the beach
    g. Shopping, running errands, or trying a new restaurant

What might you do to get out and about? Write down any ideas below.

_____

_____

_____

3. ***Engage in a nurturing self-care activity.*** By now, you can tell that this is a favorite of mine. If you are feeling depressed, it is important to send a clear message to yourself that says, "I am a valuable person. I deserve to be treated well." Treat yourself well by doing something that will make you feel cared for and soothed. As I've mentioned, some self-care activities that my patients have found helpful are:

    a. Slowing down: taking a nap or simply resting
    b. Taking a warm bath or shower
    c. Watching an uplifting movie
    d. Doing yoga, meditation, or deep breathing
    e. Going outside and enjoying nature
    f. Painting or doing anything artistic
    g. Listening to music or playing an instrument
    h. Relaxing with a good book or magazine

i. Getting a massage, facial, manicure, pedicure, or haircut

j. Buying or picking a bouquet of flowers and making some arrangements

k. Volunteering for a cause that you believe in

Now, let's pinpoint at least three self-nurturing activities that you could try this week:

_____

_____

_____

4. ***Join a support group.*** Many of my patients have found relief from depression by joining a supportive therapy group. You may find great comfort and connection in talking with others who understand your experience. Again, if you would like help in finding a therapist or support group, see page 90 for resources. Also, as previously mentioned, many of my patients have felt greatly supported by online communities they've found on websites such as ObesityHelp.com. What support groups might be of interest to you?

_____

_____

_____

5. ***Attend to your basic needs. This includes:***

a. *Getting enough sleep.* For most people, this is 7-9 hours per night. If you are struggling to get enough sleep, I encourage you to consult with your doctor. He or she can discuss both traditional and homeopathic options for improving your sleep.

b. *Eating a healthy diet.* If you are unsure of how to eat in a healthy way following your surgery, I encourage you to speak with a nutritionist. Your surgeon or primary care doctor should be able to provide you with referrals.

c. *Getting some sunlight everyday*, a practice that is associated with enhanced mood. You might try taking a short walk outdoors, having breakfast or morning coffee outside, enjoying a meal outside, or simply sitting outside in a garden or on a park bench. If you cannot get outside, I suggest that you consider purchasing a light box, which is a light that simulates sunlight and is used for the treatment of depression and seasonal affective disorder (i.e., depression that occurs during the winter months and is associated with reduced sun exposure). Ask your family doctor if he or she can recommend a specific light box that is appropriate for your needs. Your medical insurance may cover the cost.

6. ***Reach out to a family member, friend, or other loved one for support.*** If you have specific loved ones to whom you can reach out, write their names below:

_____

_____

_____

As I mentioned earlier, if you aren't able to identify anyone, you're not alone. I have learned that many post-surgery patients struggle with identifying "safe" others to reach out to for support, since they struggle to trust others or "fear being a burden." If you struggle with such feelings, I encourage you to enlist the help of a therapist. He or she can provide support and help you identify safe others with whom to share your feelings.

7. ***Consider getting a pet.*** Studies have shown that individuals with pets report greater emotional well-being than those who do not. If you're open to getting a pet, spend some time researching what type would best fit your lifestyle. Veterinarians, Humane Society volunteers, and other pet owners are great resources in the pet-choosing

process. As I mentioned earlier, many of my patients have greatly benefited from the comforting relationships they've developed with their pets. Are there any pets that you would consider getting? What resources might you tap to learn more?

_____

_____

_____

8. ***Meditate.*** As mentioned earlier, recent research strongly suggests that meditation (and the breath work done in yoga) is a highly effective tool in treating both anxiety and depression. You might consider taking a meditation or yoga class at your local YMCA, yoga studio, or fitness studio; or doing a meditation, yoga, or deep breathing DVD or CD. My meditation and relaxation CD, *Rest and Restore: Meditations and Relaxation Exercises for Stress-Relief, Mindfulness, and Peaceful Sleep* is available for digital download on iTunes, Google Play, and other major distribution outlets; and in hard-copy format at drtaniekabala.com and Amazon.com. You might also try a smartphone meditation app, which you can use almost anywhere. My meditation app, *Present and Peaceful*, is available for both Android and Apple smartphones and offers a mindfulness meditation, a walking meditation, and a five minute restorative meditation.

INACT Exercise #4: Getting Organized

Now, let's create your personalized list of strategies for addressing depression. Below, write down all of the strategies that you have identified as potentially helpful (those that you circled above). I have included five spaces, but feel free to include more:

1. _____

2. _____

3. _____

4. _____

5. _____

I hope that you now have a better understanding of any depressive feelings AND a concrete plan for addressing them. Next, let's focus on the experience of identity confusion.

CHAPTER 6

HOW TO COPE WITH IDENTITY CONFUSION

~~~&

"After the surgery, I suddenly had more opportunities:
I could fit in my car to drive, I could wear a
bathing suit. This got me asking, 'Who am I?'
and 'What do I want to do with my life?' I'd never
figured those things out. I'd never even thought
about it. I was too busy just trying to survive
everyday. Now that I'm doing more than just
surviving, I want to figure out who I really am."

-Ginny

"Who am I?" This is an extremely common question among my post-
surgery patients. Like Ginny, the majority of my patients haven't
gotten to know themselves because they've spent their energy trying to survive, fit in, gain approval, and avoid punishment. Another patient,
Suzanne, described it this way:

"I always looked to my mom for what to wear, what to say, what
to eat, what to major in....everything. I hoped if I did everything

she wanted, she'd stop criticizing me. She never did. Now I have no idea who I am or how I should be living my life. I really don't know myself and what I like.....I don't even know whether I like this jacket I'm wearing."

What Suzanne is describing is identity confusion: confusion about how to lead an **authentic** life. When I say "authentic life," I'm referring to a life that "feels right" because it reflects one's true self: one's genuine passions, preferences, opinions, wants, and needs.

Let me give another example of a patient's experience of identity confusion or "lack of authenticity." Mandy, who came to see me after her weight loss surgery and recent graduation from nursing school, gave this response when I asked her what she would like to do with her newly-acquired free time:

"I honestly don't know. I never know what to do with myself when I have free time. It gives me anxiety. I guess I should work out. I honestly don't know what I like to do. I've always just studied or watched tv."

Do you feel like Ginny, Suzanne, or Mandy? Are you unsure about your preferences, opinions, wants, needs, and passions? Are you unclear about the types of activities that give you a sense of joy or contentment? Are you uncertain about what you want and need in a friend or relationship partner? Are you unsure about "everyday things" such as what you like to wear or how you'd like to decorate your personal spaces? Are you unclear about what career is "right" for you? If your answer is "yes" to any or all of these questions, take heart- you are not alone, and although it can be challenging at times, the journey of self-discovery is an exciting one, rich with rewards. Now, let's get to the work of figuring out who you *really* are. To begin, we will use some thought-provoking questions to help you understand your personal experience of identity confusion. Then, we will do some exercises to help you identify elements of your authentic self.

INACT Exercise #1: Gaining Insight into Your Personal Experience of Identity Confusion

As we did with your feelings of loneliness, anger, anxiety, and depression, use the following pages (and feel free to use additional paper) to gain insight into your experience of identity confusion. Feel free to express anything you're feeling, using writing, drawing, a collage of pictures, or anything else that feels right. Remember, there is no wrong way to do this exercise! You can use the questions below as a guide:

* What aspects of my life feel "right?" What aspects feel "wrong?"
* Does my career feel like a good fit for me?
* What am I passionate about? Am I spending time on those passions?
* Have I lost touch with things that I used to be passionate about?
* What kind of person is a good fit for me as a friend? As a relationship partner?
* Do I dress in a way that reflects my true tastes and preferences?
* Does the décor in my personal spaces reflect my true tastes and preferences?
* What activities and experiences make me feel joyful and alive?
* What activities and experiences deplete my energy and bring me down?
* What types of people make me feel joyful and alive?
* What types of people deplete my energy and bring me down?

My Journaling Page

My Journaling Page

My Journaling Page

INACT Exercise #2: Uncovering Your Authentic Self by Learning from the Past

We can often learn a great deal about our authentic selves by reflecting on what we loved to do as children- i.e., what we loved to do before family, peer, and societal pressures took over and began steering our choices and behavior. I love to see the expression on the faces of my patients when I ask them, "What did you love to do as a child?" They generally look confused for a few moments, then smile and tell stories of authentic, fulfilling childhood experiences. Pamela, for example, looked perplexed at first when I asked her this question, then smiled and said,

> "I had forgotten about this. I loved to have my Barbie dolls put on plays. I did it everyday. I also loved being in our little school plays in elementary school. I even wrote a play in fifth grade that our class put on. I got away from it in middle school and high school though. That's when I started getting fat. I was just too self-conscious to try out or get on stage."

From this recollection, we learned that Pamela is a "theater person at heart." We used this self-knowledge to help integrate theater into her current life. She ordered season tickets to a theater company and is working on developing the courage to audition for a community theater production. By exploring the past, another patient rediscovered her love of drawing, while others have reconnected with passions for singing, dancing, building engines, making crafts, caring for animals, reading, cooking, biking, hiking, playing various sports, and birdwatching.

Now, let's turn our attention to you: what did you love to do as a child? If you were told to "go and play," what did you do? In your fondest childhood memories, what were you doing? Write down any recollections below:

_____

_____

_____

Now, take a few moments and think about how these favorite childhood activities might translate into activities that you could enjoy today. What past loves might you want to rediscover? What activities from your past might give you a sense of joy, contentment, fun, or meaning today? Write them down below:

_____

_____

_____

_____

I encourage you to try one (or all) of these activities! Write down something that you'd like to try in the near future:

_____

_____

_____

INACT Exercise #3: Uncovering Your Authentic Self by Browsing at the Bookstore

A large bookstore, such as Barnes and Noble, can be a very helpful place for those struggling with the "Who am I?" question. To help answer this question, I encourage you to browse the bookstore: give yourself unlimited time to walk *slowly* through the aisles and simply note what books, magazines, and general subject areas grab your attention. Try to relax and simply see where your natural curiosity takes you. When my patients have done this exercise, many have been surprised to find where their authenticity has led them. Suzanne said,

> "When I went to Barnes and Noble, I thought I'd just want to look at magazines, but I found myself in the fitness section look-ing at yoga books. I've guess I've been interested in that for a while but haven't tried it."

When doing this exercise, other patients have discovered authentic inter-ests in theology, gardening, scrapbooking, science fiction, Sodoku puzzles, jewelry-making, and foreign languages. As you do this exercise, take notes (either mental or written) on what you find. Write them down below:

_____

_____

_____

Now take a moment to consider how you might pursue the interest(s) you discovered in the bookstore. Some of my patients' "bookstore discoveries" have led them to read the books that caught their attention, sign up for classes, and buy supplies needed to pursue a potential hobby (e.g., gardening, jewelry-making, and scrapbooking supplies). How might you pursue the interest(s) discovered in the bookstore? Write your ideas down below:

_____

_____

_____

INACT Exercise #4: What Does the Real Me Look Like?

I remember being so struck when Suzanne said, "I don't even know whether I like this jacket I'm wearing."

Suzanne put into words a phenomenon I'd noted in so many post-surgery patients: a lack of awareness about "everyday" likes and dislikes. As I mentioned earlier, many patients have spent a lifetime adapting to the likes and dislikes of others (e.g., mothers, fathers, teachers, coaches, peers, romantic partners) in order to avoid punishment or win approval. As a result, many have not tuned into their preferences around everyday things such as:

* What styles and colors of clothes do I like?
* How would I like to wear my hair?

- Do I like makeup? If so, how much and what kind?
- Do I like jewelry? If so, how much and what kind?

The goal of the following exercises is to help you learn to reflect your authentic self through your appearance. Why is this important? Because doing so provides a sense of contentment, genuineness, and empowerment. As Georgine said,

> "I always just wore whatever fit- and whatever I could find quickly- in the plus-sized section. I'd hated to shop ever since my mom made me feel bad about buying clothes when I was fat as a kid. She liked buying clothes for my sister though. Now I'm really trying to figure out what I like. It's a little scary, but also exciting and even fun to wear things that are 'me' and make me feel pretty."

Does your appearance- such as your clothes, hairstyle, and accessories- reflect your true preferences? Or does it reflect someone else's preferences? Do you present yourself in a way that expresses yourself? Or is your presentation geared to seek approval or avoid punishment from someone else? Write down your thoughts below:

_____

_____

_____

If your appearance currently does not reflect your authentic self (and if you're not even sure what that authentic self looks like), I encourage you to try the following exercises:

a. **Start a "Things I Like Notebook."** Get some catalogs and magazines (preferably some health-oriented magazines with limited advertisements such as Natural Health) and cut out pictures of clothes, hairstyles, and accessories that appeal to you. As you look at the magazine, relax and simply see where your eye is drawn naturally. What colors do you keep coming back to? What textures, patterns, and styles? Then, tape or paste the pictures into your notebook. These images will help you answer the question "What do I like?" Make your notebook a "work in progress"- continue to paste images in as you come across them! As your notebook unfolds, write down your observations below:

_____

_____

_____

b. **Browse the department store.** As with browsing at a bookstore, take an afternoon and slowly browse the aisles of a large department store (one with many diverse styles of clothing, jewelry, and accessories). Once again, as you browse, simply see what your eye is drawn to and take note of what you find. Are there certain styles, colors, patterns, or textures of clothing that keep catching your eye? Do you find yourself drawn to hats? Scarves? Consider purchasing any items that you feel particularly drawn to, and write your observations down below:

_____

_____

_____

c. **Keep your eyes open.** As you go through your days, simply keep an eye out for styles, colors, patterns, textures, and specific items that catch your attention. Write your observations down below:

_____

_____

_____

Is it difficult for you to determine what you like? If so, please be compassionate with yourself: confronting years of messages about how you "should" present yourself and finding your authentic style can be a complex process.

If you find that doing these exercises raises challenging feelings, I encourage you to consider working with a therapist. Again, tips for finding a therapist can be found on page 90.

INACT Exercise # 5:   What Do I Love?

Another part of finding your authentic self is determining what you love to surround yourself with. Once you have figured this out, you can use the information to create personal spaces that feel "right." When our personal spaces are filled with colors, patterns, textures, and items that we love, we are filled with feelings of peace, comfort, joy, and inspiration.

As with their clothing choices, many of my patients have never reflected on what *they* love, instead building their spaces around *others'* preferences. Think about your personal spaces (e.g., your home, office, cubicle): do you like how they look and feel? Are they filled with things that you love? Do you like the colors on your walls? Your furniture? How about your window treatments and wall hangings? Is your space filled with "little things," such as decorative items or photos that you love? Are you not sure of what you love? Write your thoughts below:

_____

_____

_____

If you already feel good in your personal spaces, great! If not, I encourage you to do the exercises below to help you create spaces that reflect your authentic self and create feelings of peace and inspiration. These exercises will help you determine specifically what your personal space should look and feel like.

a. **Keep filling your "Things I Like Notebook."** This time, get some home decorating magazines and catalogs. As you browse through them, relax and simply notice what your eye is naturally drawn to. Are there certain colors, textures, patterns, and styles that you keep coming back to? Are there items that you instantly "fall in love with?"

Tape or paste the pictures of these items into your notebook, and consider purchasing any items that you feel strongly drawn to. Remember, your notebook is a "work in progress"- continue to paste images in as you come across them. As your notebook unfolds, write down your observations below:

_____

_____

_____

b. **Browse home goods stores.** Again, take an afternoon and slowly browse the aisles of a large home goods store with many diverse items (e.g., Home Goods, The World Market). Once again, as you browse, simply see what your eye is drawn to and take note of what you find. Write your observations down below, and consider purchasing any items that really speak to you:

_____

_____

_____

c. **Think about places you have loved.** Can you think of any homes, restaurants, offices, or stores that have given you a really good feeling? Is there a place where you have thought, "I just love how this looks and feels?" If so, write down below what "felt right" about them. What specifically did you love?

_____

_____

_____

Now think for a moment: what do the observations above tell you about your authentic preferences? Write your thoughts below:

_____

_____

_____

Are some authentic preferences coming into focus? If not, please try not to be discouraged: again, digging beneath years' worth of messages to excavate your true self can take time. I encourage you to keep working on the exercises above, and consider working with a therapist, trusting that your authenticity will eventually emerge. I am confident that it will!

INACT Exercise #6: Whom do YOU like?

Recently, I was sitting with one of my patients, Georgine, who was talking about a new, potential friend named Kathy. They had just had lunch together, and Georgine wondered aloud if she had made a good impression on Kathy, if she had "talked too much," if she had "said anything stupid," and if she "had anything to offer" the friendship. I asked Georgine if I could interrupt and posed the following question, "So Georgine, what do *you* think of *Kathy*?"

Georgine fell silent and looked at me rather perplexed. This is the response I get from the majority of patients when I ask them about *their* reactions to a potential friend or relationship partner. I frequently find myself saying, "You are so concerned about what they're thinking of *you* that you don't give a thought to how you're feeling with *them*." I am not encouraging my patients to be judgmental- I am simply encouraging them to carefully reflect on whether another person's personality, values, interests, wants, and needs *fit* with their personality, values, interests, wants, and needs. I have found that most of my patients do not go through this reflection process. In fact, most have no idea what type of person would be a good, healthy fit for them.

Is your experience like that of Georgine? Are you so busy worrying about what others think of *you* that you don't reflect on how you feel with *them*? Have you given any thought to what type of person would be a good fit for you in a friendship or romantic relationship? In other words, do you know what you're looking for? If not, let's figure it out together using the following exercises:

a. **With whom can I be myself, feel comfortable, and feel joy?**
Take a few moments and write down the names of people, past

and present, with whom you could be yourself, feel comfortable, and/or feel joy:

_____

_____

_____

Now, think about the characteristics of these people: how would you describe them? What are they like? What are their defining characteristics (e.g., kind, caring, compassionate, fun, loyal, artistic, understanding, thoughtful). What things are they interested in? How do they spend their time? Write your observations below:

_____

_____

_____

The information above gives us valuable data about the type of person who would likely be a good fit for you- someone who possesses at least some of the characteristics listed. As you meet people, ask yourself: does he or she possess some of these characteristics? If so, he or she might just be a good fit!

When determining if someone is a good fit for you, it is also important to know what characteristics are NOT healthy for you. Let's determine this using the following exercise:

b. **With whom do I feel uncomfortable?** Take a few moments and write down the names of people, past and present, with whom you have felt particularly anxious, uncomfortable, or distressed:

_____

_____

_____

c. Now, think about the characteristics of these people: how would you describe them? What are they like? What are their defining characteristics? What things are they interested in? How do they spend their time?

_____

_____

_____

d. Again, this information helps us understand the type of person who would likely NOT be a healthy fit for you- someone who possesses at least some of the characteristics listed. As you meet people, ask yourself: does this person possess some of these characteristics? Is this a healthy fit?

_____

_____

_____

e. **What do I want and need in a friend?** Vickie answered this question with the following statement, "I want and need someone I can trust, someone fun, a good listener who doesn't judge, someone easy-going, someone who has kids around my kids' age would be nice too, so we have that in common." What do you want and need? Write any thoughts below:

_____

_____

_____

f. **What do I want and need in a relationship partner?** For this question, Aaron said, "I want and need someone kind, caring, and affectionate. Someone who would never be verbally abusive. Someone fun who really values family." What do you want and need in a relationship partner?

_____

_____

_____

Now that you have reflected, perhaps for the first time ever, on YOUR wants, needs, and preferences in relationships, let's take a moment and summarize what you've learned:

The kind of person who would be a good fit for me in a friendship or romantic relationship would be...

_____

_____

_____

INACT Exercise #7: Getting Organized

Since we've covered so much ground in this chapter, let's take a few moments to help you organize your thoughts. Below, write down any *specific strategies* from this chapter that you'd like to continue to use in your quest to discover your authentic self (e.g., browsing the bookstore, keeping a "Things I Like" journal, reflecting on what I want/need in a friend).

_____

_____

_____

Next, record any *specific actions* that you would like to take to nurture your authentic self (e.g., revisit a certain authentic activity from childhood, wear something new that expresses your true self, buy something for your personal spaces that reflects your true tastes, reduce time spent with someone who is a "poor fit" for your authentic self).

_____

_____

_____

Before I close this chapter, I would like to briefly address one final element of identity confusion: career dissatisfaction. Many of my post-surgery patients report significant unhappiness with their jobs. Without fail, these patients have shared that they did not pursue their jobs because they were passionate about them. Instead, they took jobs because a parent, teacher, or other authority figure encouraged them to do so; because they thought the money or status of a job would make them happy; or simply because they "didn't know what else to do." The result: jobs that do not fit with the authentic self; jobs that feel meaningless, boring, and depleting; and jobs that do not inspire. Are you in such a job? If so, I encourage you to seek the assistance of a career counselor, as career counseling goes beyond the scope of this book. You can seek a career counselor at psychologytoday.com. Also, many colleges and universities offer career counseling to their graduates for a low cost. Finally, you can call local college and university counseling centers and ask for a referral to career counselors in your community.

As I close this chapter, my hope is that you are well on your way to determining who you are, what you love, and what you are looking for in relationships. Now, let's turn our attention to the compulsion to overeat.

CHAPTER 7

HOW TO COPE WITH THE URGE TO OVEREAT

⁓

"Even though I know what I "should" do
when I'm upset, sometimes I just want to
overeat, even though it makes me feel ill."

-Lori

admire you so much for coming so far in this book. By now, my hope is that you have gained some valuable insights and healthy new coping strategies. As you begin using them, please remember that just like Lori, there still might be times when you find yourself upset and compelled to overeat. If you experience this, it is *completely* normal and understandable. Just like it took time to learn to ride a bicycle, it takes time to **practice** and **learn** to cope in new ways- especially if you used an old coping technique, such as eating, for a long time. As you work on integrating your new coping strategies, I implore you to be gentle and compassionate with yourself- treat yourself as you would treat a friend who is making difficult changes!

To address the desire to overeat, I would like to introduce you to the Nourish Technique, a *mindfulness*-based technique that will allow you to avoid emotional eating and truly nourish yourself both physically and emotionally.

You might be wondering what I mean by "mindfulness." Basically, mindfulness is the act of taking a break from all of the external stimuli around you and tuning in to your *internal* experience. Applied to eating, this means taking a break from the television, cell phone, computer, kids, etc. and *really noticing* if you are hungry or not. Further, it means *really noticing* how your food looks, smells, feels, and tastes. Finally, it means *really noticing* when your body is feeling satisfied with the amount that you have eaten. To help put this concept into practice, I'd like to introduce you to the following mindfulness exercise that many of my patients have found helpful:

Mindful Eating Exercise: Eating As a Sensory Experience

To begin this mindful eating exercise, go to the kitchen and get a small serving of food, such as a few orange slices, a small handful of raisins or nuts, or a few crackers.

Step 1: Turn off any devices, such as your phone, computer, or TV. Sit in a comfortable place with the food in front of you. Close your eyes and take a few deep breaths, letting go of the outside world.

Step 2: Open your eyes and really *look* at your food. Notice the color and shape. Are there any interesting or unusual features? What do you see?

Step 3: Bring your food to your nose and *smell* it. How would you describe the aroma? Do you like it? Does it make you feel like eating the food?

Step 4: *Feel* the food in your hand. Is it heavy or light? What do you notice about the texture? Is it soft, hard, rough, or smooth?

Step 5: Now, place the food in your mouth. Notice the *taste* as the food rests on your tongue. Bite down and slowly chew. Move the food around your mouth. Really take your time, noticing every taste sensation. How would you describe the taste? Do you like it?

Step 6: When you're ready, swallow the food and notice how it feels making its way towards your stomach. Do you like the sensation? Do you feel hungry? Satisfied?

What did you notice during this exercise? Many of my patients report that they're suddenly aware of how "mindlessly" they eat, typically eating quickly and joylessly, barely noticing the experience. Also, patients frequently report that this exercise makes eating more enjoyable. Further, I often hear that it makes them feel compelled to eat *less*, because they're enjoying each bite much *more*. What were your observations?

The Nourish Technique

Mindfulness, which you just experienced in the above exercise, is the cornerstone of the Nourish Technique. As mentioned earlier, the Nourish Technique includes a series of mindfulness-based questions that help you discriminate physical from emotional hunger; and then identify either (a) what your body is truly craving or (b) what you are truly needing emotionally. Below, we will explore the steps of the Nourish Technique. Then, I will provide a handout, the Nourish Technique Guide. You can copy and use this handout whenever you need it.

The Nourish Technique: Question #1

The first question asked by the Nourish Technique is **"Am I physically hungry or emotionally hungry?"** To answer this question, first scan your body for signs of *physical* hunger: does your stomach feeling empty or hollow? Do you feel weak or dizzy? Are you mildly nauseous? Is your stomach growling? It might help to close your eyes as you're scanning for these physical sensations of hunger. Take your time, relax, and really listen to your body. The Nourish Technique Guide provides space to record your observations.

Next, tune into signs of *emotional* hunger. Close your eyes, take a few deep breaths, and attend to your internal experience. Do you notice any feelings of sadness, anxiety, anger, or loneliness? Do you feel agitated or "at loose ends?" Are you bored? Tired? Do you feel like yelling, crying, or just going to sleep? Are you engaging in any "nervous habits," such as biting your fingernails or bobbing your leg? Again, the Nourish Technique Guide provides space to record your observations.

The Nourish Technique: Question #2

If your answer to Question #1 ("Am I physically hungry or emotionally hungry?") is *physically hungry*, then ask yourself Nourish Technique Question #2: **"What is my body truly craving?"**

Bearing in mind any post-surgery dietary restrictions, think carefully about the foods listed below and *actually imagine yourself eating them.* How would they feel in your body? Which one(s) is your *body* craving in order to feel nourished right now? If you truly listen to your body, you will find that it craves a healthy combination of the food groups listed below:

Dairy (e.g., yogurt, cottage cheese, a yogurt smoothie, a cheese stick)
Fruits (e.g., oranges, grapes, apples, bananas)
Vegetables (e.g., salad, carrots, broccoli)
Protein (e.g., nuts, eggs, peanut butter, beans, meat)
Carbohydrates (e.g., bread, cereal, pasta)
Whole grains (e.g., whole grain bread, crackers, or cereal)
Salty foods (e.g., pretzels)
Sweet foods (e.g., dark chocolate)
Liquids, as thirst is often mistaken for hunger (e.g., water, fruit or vegetable juice, milk)

Take a moment to list below some foods (or food combinations) from these groups that are likely to satisfy you when you're physically hungry. Some examples include cottage cheese with fruit, peanut butter on whole grain bread, salad with turkey and cheese, cereal with milk, a fruit and yogurt smoothie, a bean and cheese burrito. I encourage you to add to this list as you make new discoveries.

_____

_____

_____

Once you have identified what your body is craving, *mindfully* eat *whatever* you are craving until you feel *satisfied*. Many patients are daunted by this statement, saying things like, "I can't be trusted to eat some of the foods on that list!" and, "I'll pig out if I let myself have peanut butter!"

How can you trust yourself to eat what you're truly craving until you're satisfied? In my experience, mindful eating is the key. As you engage in a mindful eating practice (using the exercise on page 78 as a guide), you will find that your body and mind have all of the wisdom needed to (a) eat a healthy combination of foods and (b) stop when you're satisfied. My patients frequently report that when they begin eating mindfully, they are shocked by the types of foods that they crave- foods that they had never cared about before. I recall one of my patients saying, "I had never bought an orange in my life before I started eating mindfully. I thought they were just annoying health food. Now I keep them around all the time- I crave them a lot and really love them." Also, patients are often surprised by how much *less* they're compelled to eat when eating mindfully.

As you practice mindful eating, I deeply encourage you to be patient and compassionate with yourself. As I said earlier, just like learning to ride a bike, learning to eat mindfully takes time and practice. You might have moments of frustration and self-criticism. In those moments, please try to stop, take a breath, put your hand on your heart, and say some encouraging, compassionate words to yourself. One of my patients likes to say, "You're working hard at this and I'm proud of you." Another says, "This is really hard, but you can do it. Take it one day at a time." What might you say to yourself in moments of frustration or self-criticism? Write your ideas below:

_____

_____

_____

As my patients are learning to eat mindfully until they are satisfied, I also often hear the question, "What does satisfied even mean? I can never find the happy medium between unsatisfied and stuffed!" How can you determine when you're satisfied? My favorite way to determine this is to ask yourself this question: do you have a sense of fullness, but still could get up and comfortably dance? Similarly, you might ask yourself, "Do I have a sense of fullness, but still could get up and comfortably take a brisk walk?" As you're mindfully eating a meal, periodically check-in with yourself and ask yourself one of these questions.

The Nourish Technique: Question #3

If your answer to Question #1 was *emotionally hungry*, then ask yourself Question #3: "**What am I feeling and needing emotionally right now?**" Again, close your eyes, take a deep breath, and tune into your emotional world. What are you feeling and needing right now? Are you feeling lonely, anxious, angry, or depressed? Are you agitated? Do you feel bored? Tired? Do you need support, connection with others, rest, relaxation, sleep, nurturing, or to express a feeling such as anger? Let your feelings wash over you- really experience and notice them. On the Nourish Technique Guide, you will find a space to record your observations.

The Nourish Technique: Question #4

If your answer to Question #1 was *emotionally hungry*, then ask yourself Question #4: "**What can I do right now to soothe myself that does not involve food?**" Look back at the coping strategies you've developed thus far in our book for guidance. Do you just need to slow down, lie down, and get some rest or sleep? Would it help to write in your journal? Get out of the house and take a walk, go to a store, or exercise? Call or visit a friend or loved one? Watch a favorite movie? Take a step towards resolving an issue with a friend, family member, or co-worker? Again, the Nourish Technique Guide on the following page provides space for you to record all of your observations. As I mentioned earlier, please feel free to copy and use it whenever needed.

The Nourish Technique Guide
Tanie Miller Kabala, Ph.D.

To feed your body what it needs and avoid emotional eating, walk yourself through the following mindfulness-based questions:

QUESTION #1: Am I physically hungry or emotionally hungry?

Determine this by scanning your body for signs of physical hunger, such as a hollow feeling in your stomach, weakness, dizziness, or nausea. Also scan for signs of emotional hunger: feelings of sadness, anxiety, anger, boredom, loneliness, or agitation; or the desire to yell, cry, or go to sleep. Do your best to determine the type of hunger you're experiencing and record it in the space below:

If the answer to Question #1 was *physically hungry*, then ask yourself Question #2:

QUESTION #2: What is my body craving?

Try to determine what food group(s) your body needs right now. Think carefully about the foods listed below- imagine eating them- and ask which ones your body needs in order to feel nourished right now:

Dairy (e.g., yogurt, cheese, smoothie)   Fruits (e.g., oranges, grapes, apples)
Vegetables (e.g., broccoli, carrots, salad) Protein (e.g., nuts, eggs, peanut butter, meat)
Carbohydrates (e.g., bread, cereal, pasta) Whole grains (e.g., bread, crackers, or cereal)
Salty foods (e.g., pretzels)   Sweet foods (e.g., dark chocolate)

Liquids, as thirst is often mistaken for hunger (e.g., water, fruit or vegetable juice, milk)

Now, mindfully eat *whatever* food your body is craving until you feel *satisfied*. I like to say that you are "satisfied" when you have a sense of fullness, but still could comfortably dance or walk briskly.

Bearing in mind any post-surgery dietary restrictions, eat whatever your body is asking for. Avoid having "forbidden" foods. As you follow this practice, you will find that you desire a healthy combination of the food groups listed above.

If your answer to Question #1 was *emotionally hungry*, then ask yourself Questions #3 and #4:

QUESTION #3: What am I feeling and needing emotionally right now?

Are you feeling lonely, anxious, angry, or depressed? Are you agitated? Bored? Tired? Do you need support, connection with others, rest, relaxation, nurturing, or to express a feeling to someone? Let your feelings wash over you- really notice them- and then write your experience below:

QUESTION #4: What can I do right now to feel better that does not involve food?

Would it help to get together with someone, get out of the house, write in a journal, take a nap, or watch a movie? Look back at the coping strategies you've developed thus far in our book for guidance. Write your ideas below:

I recognize that walking through the steps of the Nourish Technique can feel like a lot of work, both mental and emotional. If you really don't want to overeat, but are simply too exhausted or overwhelmed to use it, I encourage you to try any of the quick, simple techniques in my COPE strategy:

1. **C**hange your environment: Overeating is often triggered by something or someone in your immediate environment (e.g., the stress of work, the boredom of being home alone, the distress of having had an argument with a family member). Therefore, it is often helpful to change your environment the minute you feel compelled to overeat. Go to a store that you like, take a walk, visit someone, or simply go outside for some fresh air and a change of scenery. Remember, the urge will eventually pass!

2. **O**pen up to someone: Overeating is usually driven by painful or challenging feelings, so if you feel this compulsion, call or visit a loved one and *share* your experience. You might also consider joining an online forum, such as ObesityHelp.com, where you can seek the support and encouragement of other post-surgery patients. Take these opportunities to vent your feelings and gain support. Again, the urge *will* pass.

3. **P**ray, meditate, or do some breathing exercises: When you feel compelled to overeat, diffuse the energy by stopping what you're doing, going to a quiet place (one of my patients even resorted to going to the bathroom at work), and engaging in a centering activity such as prayer, meditation, or deep breathing. These activities soothe, comfort, and clear the mind- exactly what you need when you feel compelled to overeat. You can find my Five Minute Meditation script on page 93.

4. **Exercise:** As Amy put it, "The second I feel an urge to overeat coming on, I put on my sneakers and start walking." Amy, like many of my patients, finds that exercise provides a healthy diversion from the overeating compulsion. It also releases endorphins (which boost mood), clears the mind, and bolsters self-esteem.

Now, write down below the parts of the COPE technique that would likely work best for you:

_____
_____
_____

I truly hope that you feel well-prepared to care for yourself when confronted with the urge to overeat. Now, let's take all the strategies that you've identified in the previous chapters and put them in your quick reference guide, or "Coping Companion."

CHAPTER 8

PUTTING IT ALL TOGETHER: YOUR COPING COMPANION

‚Äî‚ò∞‚Äî

truly hope that our work has helped you understand your feelings and identify useful, food-free strategies for coping with them effectively. Because
we've covered so much ground, you might want to take a few moments
to create an organized, easy-to-access reference guide- your own "Coping
Companion" that you can flip to quickly and easily when you need it. You
can use the spaces below to transfer the strategies that you identified in each
of the chapters we've completed:

My strategies for coping with loneliness (page 21):

My strategies for coping with anger (page 35):

My strategies for coping with anxiety (page 49):

My strategies for coping with depression (page 57):

My strategies for coping with identity confusion (page 75):

My strategies for coping with the urge to overeat (pages 84-86):

Great job! As I said at the beginning of our journey, I'm so glad that you took this important step in self care following your surgery. I truly hope that this work serves you not only in the weeks and months following your surgery, but for a lifetime. Wishing you all the best!

Tips for Finding a Therapist

I'm so glad that you're considering finding a therapist. Here are some strategies for locating a good therapist near you:

1. **Visit Psychologytoday.com.** This web site has a "find a therapist" function which allows you to type in your zip code and view the profiles of therapists near you. Profiles include information about each therapist's therapeutic style, location, fees, and insurances accepted.

2. **Ask your surgeon, primary care physician, or OB/GYN for a referral.** Most physicians have the names and numbers of local therapists readily available.

3. **Call a local college or university counseling center** and ask for referrals for private practice therapists in the community. Most college and university counseling centers maintain a list of local therapists and are happy to provide referrals.

4. **Network with family and friends.** If you feel comfortable, ask family members and friends if they can refer you to a good therapist.

5. **Ask your pastor, priest, rabbi, or other spiritual/religious leader for a referral.** Many such leaders keep the names and numbers of local therapists readily available.

Best of luck to you!

Progressive Muscle Relaxation Script

The following script can be used anytime you need to relax your body, mind and spirit. You can have someone read the script to you (this will allow you to close your eyes), read the script to yourself, or make a recording of your voice (or someone else's) reading the script. Enjoy!

Begin by finding a comfortable position either sitting or lying down. You can change positions at any point during the progressive muscle relaxation exercise to make yourself more comfortable.

Begin by taking a deep breath: breathe in…...hold it for a moment…and now release. Take three more deep breaths at your own pace, releasing all of your tension as you exhale.

Now continue to breathe naturally for five to ten breaths, allowing your breath to relax you.

Now we'll focus on relaxing the muscles of your body:

Let's start with the large muscles of your legs. Tighten all of the muscles of your legs. Keep holding this tension. Feel how tight and tense the muscles feel. Squeeze your leg muscles even harder. Notice how the muscles want to give up the tension. Hold it for a few moments more.... and now relax, letting all of the tension go. Feel the muscles in your legs relaxing, loosening, going limp. Notice the difference between tension and relaxation in your legs. Enjoy the pleasant feeling of relaxation.

Take three deep breaths.

Now, let's focus on the muscles of your buttocks. Tighten these muscles. Hold the tension….keep holding. Again, notice how the muscles want to give up the tension…and now relax. Let all of the tension go. Enjoy the pleasant feeling of relaxation.

Note the rhythmic pace of your breath.

Now, let's focus on the muscles of your arms and hands. Tighten your shoulders, upper arms, lower arms, and hands. Make tight fists with your hands. Hold the tension....keep holding.....feel the tension. Hold it for a few moments more.... and now relax, letting all of the tension go. Let the muscles of your shoulders, arms, and hands go loose and limp. Enjoy the feeling of relaxation as you relax these muscles.

Now, turn your attention to the muscles of your chest and stomach. Tighten these muscles....keep tightening them....hold this tension....notice how the tension feels....and now release. Feel the relaxation. Notice the tension leaving your body.

Take three deep breaths.

Next, tighten the muscles of your back. Pull your shoulders back and arch your back slightly as you tense all the muscles along your spine. Hold.... keep holding.....feel the tension.....and relax. Let all of the tension go. Note the pleasant difference between tension and relaxation.

Finally, tighten all of the muscles of your face. Close your eyes tightly, scrunch up your nose, and smile widely. Hold this tension in your face.... keep holding....a little tighter now....and relax. Let all of the tension go. Notice the feeling of relaxation in your face.

Now, scan your body. Is there any place that you still feel tension? If so, take a moment to tighten and release that muscle or muscle group. Tighten that muscle.....keep holding....tighten it a little bit more.....and release. Feel the relaxation.

Now, notice how your body feels all over. Notice the heavy, loose, relaxed feeling of your muscles. Enjoy this moment. Notice your calm breathing.... your relaxed body. Take a few more moments just to enjoy this feeling.

When you feel ready, slowly begin to re-awaken your body. Open your eyes, wiggle your toes and fingers, and shrug your shoulders.

Take three more deep, calming breaths.

Your progressive muscle relaxation exercise is now complete.

I hope that this exercise has left you feeling relaxed, refreshed, and rejuvenated!

Five Minute Meditations

I Am Relaxed. For this breath work, sit comfortably, close your eyes, and breathe in and out normally. On your inhale, silently recite, "I am..." and on your exhale, recite, "relaxed." You may use any other mantra that is meaningful to you. Some mantras my clients have used are, "Healing in (on the inhalation)......pain out (on the exhalation)," and "Love in (to self).....love out (to others)." Whenever your mind wanders, just notice it and non-judgmentally come back to the mantra. Continue for five minutes. End with three deep, calming breaths.

Breath Attention. For this practice, sit comfortably, close your eyes, and breathe in and out normally. Simply pay attention to your breath. Note where you feel the breath in your body. Do you feel it filling your lungs? Do you feel it in your belly? Leaving your nostrils? Whenever your mind wanders, just notice it and non-judgmentally return to attending to your breath. Continue for five minutes. End with three deep, calming breaths.

Five Senses Meditation. For this practice, sit comfortably and close your eyes. Take five to ten calming breaths. Breathe in through your nose and out through your mouth. On the inhale, silently say to yourself, "I am." On the exhale, say to yourself, "Relaxed." Next, take a minute to notice each of your five senses. Say to yourself:

"I hear _____" Simply notice the sounds around you.

"I feel _____" Simply notice any physical sensations in your body.

"I smell _____" Simply notice any smells in the air.

"I taste _____" Simply notice any tastes in your mouth.

"I see _____" Open your eyes and notice what you see around you.

Repeat as many times as you'd like. Finish with three deep, calming breaths.

The Nourish Technique Guide
Tanie Miller Kabala, Ph.D.

To feed your body what it needs and avoid emotional eating, walk yourself through the following mindfulness-based questions:

QUESTION #1: Am I physically hungry or emotionally hungry?

Determine this by scanning your body for signs of physical hunger, such as a hollow feeling in your stomach, weakness, dizziness, or nausea. Also scan for signs of emotional hunger: feelings of sadness, anxiety, anger, boredom, loneliness, or agitation; or the desire to yell, cry, or go to sleep. Do your best to determine the type of hunger you're experiencing and record it in the space below:

If the answer to Question #1 was *physically hungry*, then ask yourself Question #2:

QUESTION #2: What is my body craving?

Try to determine what food group(s) your body needs right now. Think carefully about the foods listed below- imagine eating them- and ask which ones your body needs in order to feel nourished right now:

Dairy (e.g., yogurt, cheese, smoothie)
Fruits (e.g., oranges, grapes, apples)
Vegetables (e.g., broccoli, carrots, salad)
Protein (e.g., nuts, eggs, peanut butter, meat)
Carbohydrates (e.g., bread, cereal, pasta)
Whole grains (e.g., bread, crackers, or cereal)
Salty foods (e.g., pretzels)

Sweet foods (e.g., dark chocolate)
Liquids, as thirst is often mistaken for hunger (e.g., water, fruit or vegetable juice, milk)

Now, mindfully eat *whatever* food your body is craving until you feel *satisfied*. I like to say that you are "satisfied" when you have a sense of fullness, but still could comfortably dance or walk briskly.

Bearing in mind any post-surgery dietary restrictions, eat whatever your body is asking for. Avoid having "forbidden" foods. As you follow this practice, you will find that you desire a healthy combination of the food groups listed above.

If your answer to Question #1 was *emotionally hungry*, then ask yourself Questions #3 and #4:

QUESTION #3: What am I feeling and needing emotionally right now?

Are you feeling lonely, anxious, angry, or depressed? Are you agitated? Bored? Tired? Do you need support, connection with others, rest, relaxation, nurturing, or to express a feeling to someone? Let your feelings wash over you- really notice them- and then write your experience below:

QUESTION #4: What can I do right now to feel better that does not involve food?

Would it help to get together with someone, get out of the house, write in a journal, take a nap, or watch a movie? Look back at the coping strategies you've developed thus far in our book for guidance. Write your ideas below:

Mindful Eating Exercise:
Eating As a Sensory Experience

To begin this mindful eating exercise, go to the kitchen and get a small serving of food, such as a few orange slices, a small handful of raisins or nuts, or a few crackers.

Step 1: Turn off any devices, such as your phone, computer, or TV. Sit in a comfortable place with the food in front of you. Close your eyes and take a few deep breaths, letting go of the outside world.

Step 2: Open your eyes and really *look* at your food. Notice the color and shape. Are there any interesting or unusual features? What do you see?

Step 3: Bring your food to your nose and *smell* it. How would you describe the aroma? Do you like it? Does it make you feel like eating the food?

Step 4: *Feel* the food in your hand. Is it heavy or light? What do you notice about the texture? Is it soft, hard, rough, or smooth?

Step 5: Now, place the food in your mouth. Notice the *taste* as the food rests on your tongue. Bite down and slowly chew. Move the food around your mouth. Really take your time, noticing every taste sensation. How would you describe the taste? Do you like it?

Step 6: When you're ready, swallow the food and notice how it feels making its way towards your stomach. Do you like the sensation? Do you feel hungry? Satisfied?

What did you notice during this exercise?

ABOUT THE AUTHOR

—6

D r. Tanie Miller Kabala received psychology training at Georgetown University, George Washington University, George Mason University, and the University of Delaware. She earned her Ph.D. with honors in 2003 and has practiced psychology in multiple settings, including community mental health centers and university counseling centers. Dr. Kabala currently works in private practice, where she specializes in treating individuals before and after weight loss surgery. She travels the country speaking to weight loss surgery patients, support groups, and medical professionals about healthy coping after surgery. Dr. Kabala also has a passion for using meditation and relaxation exercises to help her patients experience increased emotional and physical well-being. She enjoys offering meditation and relaxation classes to her community.

Please feel free to visit Dr. Kabala's website at www.drtaniekabala.com, or follow her on Facebook (https://www.facebook.com/drtaniekabala) or Twitter (https://twitter.com/drtaniekabala).

33397689R00062

Made in the USA
Middletown, DE
12 July 2016